When I Read

MY Bible

Children FLY High Series

Gwendolyn Rosemary Davis-King

To order additional copies of this book, contact:
Xlibris
1-888-795-4274
www.Xlibris.com
Orders@Xlibris.com

WHEN I READ MY BIBLE

DEDICATION

In Loving Memory

Of MY Beloved Sister
*

Barbara Ann Maxwell

WHEN I READ MY BIBLE

BEFORE GOING TO SCHOOL

IT REMINDS ME THAT I

CAN FOLLOW EVERY RULE.

WHEN I READ MY BIBLE

BEFORE PERFORMING A CLASS SOLO...

IT TAKES AWAY THE FEAR

SO MY WORDS WILL SIMPLY FLOW.

WHEN I READ MY BIBLE

BEFORE ATTENDING CHURCH MASS...

IT HELPS ME TO ANSWER QUESTIONS

IN MY SUNDAY SCHOOL CLASS.

WHEN I READ MY BIBLE

BEFORE GOING OUT TO PLAY...

IT TEACHES ME TO BE KIND

IN WHAT I DO AND SAY.

WHEN I READ MY BIBLE

BEFORE GOING TO BED...

IT MAKES ME AWAKE HAPPY

WITH GOOD THOUGHTS IN MY HEAD.

WHEN I READ MY BIBLE

LEARNING MORE ABOUT GOD'S SON

IT MAKES ME WANT TO BE LIKE HIM

WHO LOVED EVERYONE.

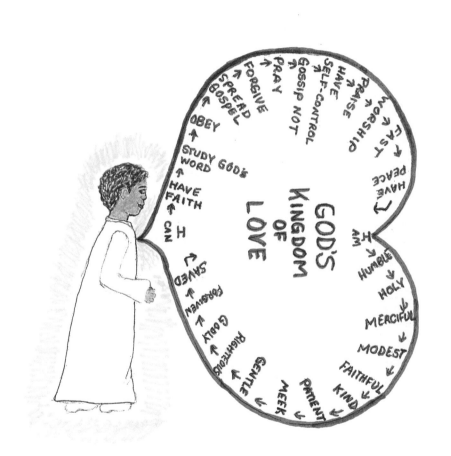

WHEN I READ MY BIBLE

BEING ALL JESUS WANTS ME TO BE...

HE PROMISES THAT I WILL LIVE WITH HIM

IN HEAVEN ETERNALLY.

SPEAK GREEK

But Jesus called them unto Him, and said, Suffer little children to come unto me, and forbid them not: for of such is the Kingdom of God.   Saint Luke 18:16

Ὁ δε Ἰησους προσεκαλέσατο αυτὰ λέγων, Ἄφετε τὰ παιδία ἔρχεσθαι πρός με καὶ μη κωλύετε αὐτά, των γὰρ τοιού- των εστὶν ἡ βασιλεία του θεου.   ΚΑΤΑ ΛΟΥΚΑΝ 18:16

Ha de E-a-soos pro-se-ka-<u>le</u>-sa-toe ow-ta leg-own, A-fe-te ta
Lg lg sh   sh   sh   sh sh sh lg   sh sh   sh   lg   sh sh sh sh

pie-di-a εr-kes-thi pros mε ki may ko-loo-e-te, tone gar
lg sh sh sh sh   lg   sh   sh lg lg lg sh sh sh   lg   sh

toy-oo- tone es-tin hay Ba-see-le-yah too Thay-u.   ΚΑΤΑ ΛΟΥΚΑΝ 18:16
lg   sh   lg   sh sh lg   sh   lg sh sh lg   lg   KA-TA LU-CAN
                                                                            Sh Sh Lg Sh

Vowels sounds are: long = lg or short = sh
Many Greek double vowels make one sound which is called a "dipthong."
Example: ai <u>ai</u>sle, oi t<u>oi</u>l, ei <u>ei</u>ght

GREEK ALPHABET

Alpha	αλφα	a	A	α	Family
Beta	βήτα	b	B	β	boy
Gamma	γαμμα	g	Γ	γ	glow
Delta	δέλτα	d	Δ	δ	door
Epsilon	εφιλόν	e	E	ε	Esther
Zeta	ζητα	z	Z	ζ	amaze
Eta	ητα	a	H	η	obey
Theta	θητα	th	Θ	θ	think
Iota	ιωτα	i	I	ι	sing
Kappa	κάππα	k	K	κ	kind
Lambda	λάμβδα	l	Λ	λ	love
Mu	μυ	m	M	μ	mighty
Nu	νυ	n	N	ν	name
Xi	ξι	x	Ξ	ξ	maximum
Omicron	ομικρόν	o	O	o	God
Pi	πι	p	Π	π	piece
Rho	ρω	r	P	ρ	ring
Sigma	σίγμα	s	Σ	σ/ς	safe
Tau	ταυ	t	T	τ	teach
Upsilon	υψιλόν	u/y	Y	υ	wound
Phi	φι	ph	Φ	φ	pharaoh
Chi	χι	ch	X	χ	character
Psi	ψι	ps	Ψ	ψ	grips
Omega	ωμέγα	o	Ω	ω	stone

WHEN I READ MY BIBLE

When I read my Bible
Before going to school...
It reminds me that I
Can follow every rule.

When I read my Bible
Before performing a class solo...
It takes away the fear
So my words will simply flow.

When I read my Bible
Before attending Church Mass...
It helps me to answer questions
In my Sunday School class.

When I read my Bible
Before going out to play...

It teaches me how to be kind
In what I do and say.

When I read my Bible
Before going to bed...
It makes me wake up happy
With good thoughts in my head.

When I read my Bible
Learning more about God's Son
It makes me want to be like Him
Who loved everyone.

When I read my Bible
Being all Jesus wants me to be...
He promises that I will live with Him
In heaven eternally.

By Gwendolyn Rosemary Davis-King

CHILDREN FLY HIGH CENTER OF THOUGHT

ATTITUDE CHECK!
Which answer is true?

a. _____ Reading the Bible is not more important than doing my home work.
b. _____ Reading the Bible is for grownups.
c. _____ Jesus does not mind if I do not read my Bible since He loves me.
d. _____ If I really love Jesus, I will read my Bible and obey God's Word.

What Should I Do?
Let's Make Jesus Smile!

1. If my friend asks to take my ball home to play with it but does not bring it back to me, what should I do?
_____Beat him down for not returning it
_____Should not ask for it back, but give him my bat as well.

2. If a group of children call me names because I read my Bible, what should I do?
_____stick my tongue out at them
_____Pray for them

3. When my wealthy friend comes to Sunday-School with his hair uncombed and bagging pants and laughs about it, what should I do?
_____ignore him since he is behaving unseemly
_____Tell him how much Jesus loves him and wants to come into his heart.

What Do You Know About the Bible?
Quiz

1. How many books are in the Bible?
a. 50
b. 100
c. 66

2. What are the first five books of the Bible called?
a. bible books
b. torah or law
c. stories

3. What is the Bible?
a. a heavy thick book that is hard to carry
b. a good book
c. the Word of God

4. The Bible is divided into two parts. What are they called?
a. Testament
b. Old Testament
c. Old and New Testament

5. Who wrote the first five books of the Old Testament?
a. Moses
b. James
c. Obadiah

*Does reading your Bible make you rich? yes_____ no_____ Selah!

WORD FIND

Have fun!

Do you know who Jesus is? Write "Jesus is Love!" in the top squares.

C	O	M	M	A	N	D	M	E	N	T	E
L	L	A	A	W	A	R	B	B	P	Y	T
A	O	S	N	O	W	O	I	E	L	D	E
S	S	S	K	N	O	B	S	D	A	E	R
S	Y	S	I	K	L	A	O	E	Y	T	N
N	O	O	N	E	F	G	H	K	A	W	A
S	U	N	D	A	Y	S	C	H	O	O	L

Circle words found.

a. mass
b. know
c. book
d. two
e. flow

f. eternal
g. bed
h. play
i. head
j. man

k. commandment
l. class
m. read
n. Son
o. Godly

p. Bible
q. Sunday School
r. no one
s. kind
t. An

WHEN YOU GIVE YOUR WHOLE HEART TO JESUS,

HE WILL GUIDE YOU TO READ 'THE BIBLE.'

Psalm 119:1-4

119 Blessed are the undefiled in the way, who walk in the law of the Lord.

2 Blessed are they that keep his testimonies, and that seek him with the whole heart.

3 They also do no iniquity: they walk in his ways.

4 Thou hast commanded us to keep thy precepts diligently.

Psalm 119:105-108

105 Thy word is a lamp unto my feet, and a light unto my path.

106 I have sworn, and I will perform it, that I will keep thy righteous judgments.

107 I am afflicted very much: quicken me, O Lord, according unto thy word.

108 Accept, I beseech thee, the freewill offerings of my mouth, O Lord, and teach me thy judgments.

READING THE BIBLE IS...'FLYING HIGH'

THE END!

Printed in the United States
By Bookmasters